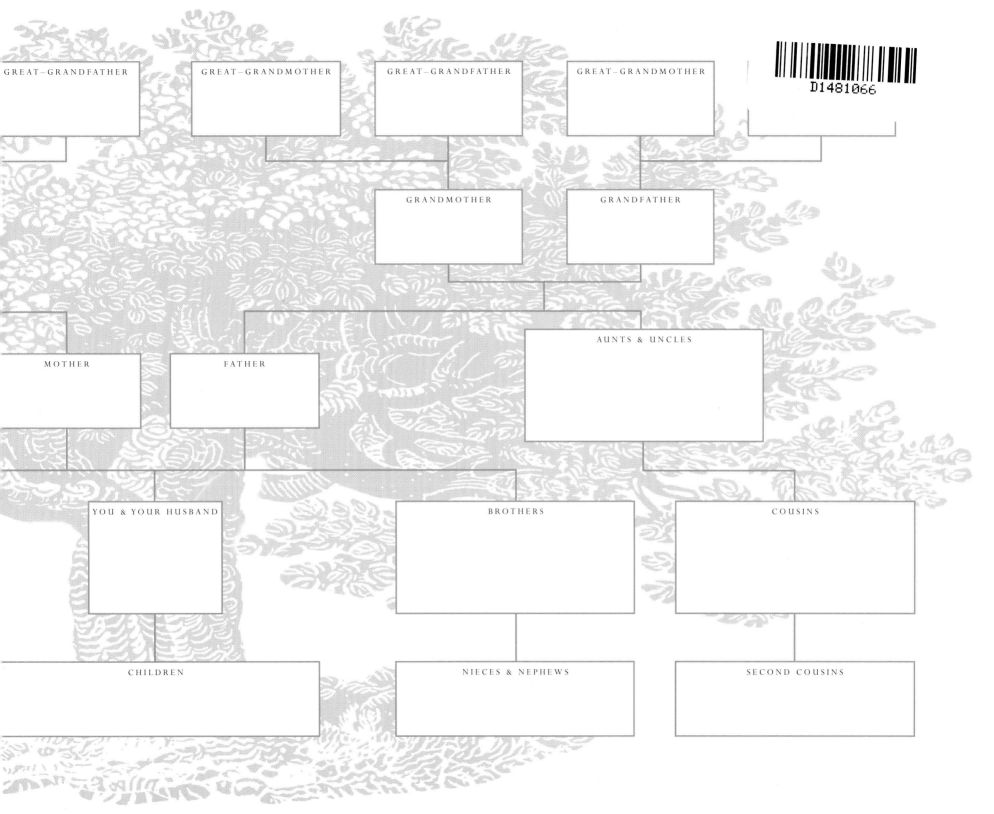

GREAT–GRANDFATHER

GREAT–GRANDMOTHER

GREAT–GRANDFATHER

GREAT–GRANDMOTHER

GRANDMOTHER

GRANDFATHER

AUNTS & UNCLES

MOTHER

FATHER

YOU & YOUR HUSBAND

BROTHERS

COUSINS

CHILDREN

NIECES & NEPHEWS

SECOND COUSINS

MILLENNIUM
FAMILY TREE
— RECORD BOOK —

DK PUBLISHING, INC.
www.dk.com

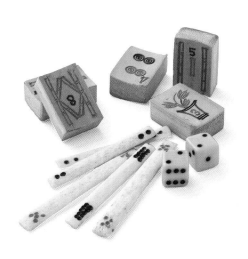

MILLENNIUM FAMILY TREE

Every family has its history, but never in history has our definition of what constitutes a family been so flexible. We understand families to be a set of relations, usually parents and children, or to be members of one household. However, on the brink of a new millennium, the "rules" governing the definition of the family are ever-changing. Nuclear families of two parents living with their children, who are in regular contact with the extended family of grandparents, aunts, uncles and cousins, are not always the norm. Stepfamilies are increasingly common, as are families with single parents.

But families are changing, not disappearing. There is still a need for a family identity, and the need for knowledge of the people who make up a family's past is fundamental – it is at the heart of storytelling the world over. Many people are fascinated to know the story of where they have come from. While family structures may be more versatile than in the past, and their members more mobile, methods of tracing and recording family histories are becoming more sophisticated and more accessible. With patience and help from sources such as family members, public records, genealogical societies, and now the Internet, everyone has a chance of being able to trace the threads of that story.

If you are fascinated by your family's history, you need to start keeping a record of what you already know. This *Millennium Family Tree Record Book* will help you do that. And if you are tempted to turn detective, what better time is there to record your own family history than at the landmark of the new millennium? A new millennium is a symbolic date for bringing together everything that you know so far, and for future generations it is a historic date to look back at. Once your family tree has been brought up to date, you will be able to add to it and follow it through for the future. As part of your research you could compare notes and share anecdotes with other members of your family; you may find that you end up with more facts and richer stories than you would have discovered on your own.

It is certain that for decades to come your children, grandchildren and great-grandchildren will want to know about their family before and at the new millennium. With this record book they can look back into the previous millennium and forward into the new millennium, and they will have all the information they need at their fingertips.

A DK PUBLISHING BOOK
www.dk.com

Design and text Mason Linklater
Managing Art Editor Philip Gilderdale
Managing Editor Jemima Dunne
Senior Art Editor Karen Ward
Production Antony Heller

Special photography David Merewether
Border illustration Jane Thomson

Millennium edition published in 2000

2 4 6 8 10 9 7 5 3 1

Published in the United States by
DK Publishing, Inc.
95 Madison Avenue
New York NY 10016

Published in Great Britain by Dorling Kindersley Limited.

ISBN 0-7894-2076-7

Color reproduction by Colorlito Rigogliosi S.R.L., Milan, Italy
Printed and bound by Tien Wah Press, Singapore

ACKNOWLEDGMENTS
Dorling Kindersley would like to thank the following for supplying items for special photography: Gunvor Avery and Ingrid Mason. The following photographs were reproduced by courtesy of London Toy and Model Museum, pages 12, 22, 29; Mattel UK Ltd., page 13; Faith Eaton Collection, pages 22, 40, 55; Worthing Museum and Art Gallery, page 24; Judy Sparrow, page 28; LawleysLtd, page 37; Paul and Rosemary Volpp, page 46; National Maritime Museum, page 47. Dorling Kindersley would like to thank the following for their kind permission to reproduce their photographs: Pictor International: L. Paul Mann p2/3.

TRACING YOUR FAMILY TREE

Where would we be without our families and the life we enjoy with them? Family gives us stability and reassurance in a world of rapid change. It applauds our triumphs and achievements without envy, bears with us when times are hard, and is the mainstay in celebrating landmark events throughout our lives. Family is about continuity, knowing where we have come from and seeing where we are going.

Every family has its unique characteristics – whether of intellect, looks, or temperament – that pass from one generation to the next. When we look into the past, we see members of our family mirrored in generations gone by (Mom has her father's eyes; Dad has Grandma's amazing memory); when we observe the present and look forward into the future, we see ourselves reflected in our children.

Setting out on your search

In constructing a family tree, a skillful, seasoned genealogist is able to trace the direct line of descent through many generations, covering hundreds of years with probably thousands of names. Such a search is not only time-consuming but also costly; as an alternative, you can set out on your search with the more modest and achievable aim of compiling the family tree (or "pedigree," as it is known) of your most recent ancestors. Cataloging the accumulated knowledge of your parents should enable you to trace your family tree back as far as your great-grandparents' generation, on both your mother's and your father's side. In the process, you may even turn up long-lost or far-flung relatives who will provide vital clues for research into more distant times.

Sources of information: family stories & papers

First decide whether to trace your maternal and paternal lines at the same time. Tracing both lines simultaneously will not affect the result, but you may find it less complicated to complete your research into one line before starting on the other. Let family members know that you are researching your family tree, and enlist their help to gather as much information as possible, especially details of marriages and children, plus any family stories that they would like to contribute. Sketch out a rough family tree that shows each generation on a separate level, and keep in a series of notebooks or computer files a meticulous record of every piece of information you discover. Plan on updating these regularly — and your sketch — as new information emerges, and do not

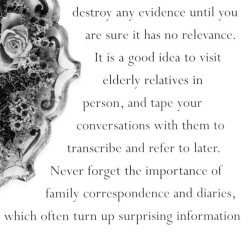

destroy any evidence until you are sure it has no relevance. It is a good idea to visit elderly relatives in person, and tape your conversations with them to transcribe and refer to later. Never forget the importance of family correspondence and diaries, which often turn up surprising information (for example, details of illegitimate children or divorces) that sensitive relatives may be unwilling to reveal.

Matters of public record

Occasionally, you may need to test the accuracy of information sourced from family members, in particular elderly ones; or perhaps some line of enquiry will prove inconclusive. This is the time to consider moving on to a more serious level of research: consulting public records. Certificates of birth and marriage are your starting point, and although details vary from one region and time period to another, the basic information is the same. A birth certificate records the individual's name, parents (including the mother's maiden name and the father's occupation), and the date and place of birth. A marriage certificate shows the names of the couple (and their fathers' names), residence and age when married, and the date and place of the ceremony. Wills, census reports, and parochial and civil records also yield useful information. For this level of research, it is well worth joining your local historical or genealogical society, which can guide you through the complicated maze of the public record system.

An heirloom for future generations

Taking time to trace your family tree is an opportunity to gather your own treasury of remembrance, memento, and fact. You will probably find that you become more and more engrossed in your searches as you discover new leads, pursuing them from one part of the country to another (even to other continents) to bring together all the rich detail of your family's history and your partner's.

As your quest reveals each new name, write it in your notebook and then go on with your research. Remember, especially if your surname is not unusual, that a name must be verified with biographical detail that clearly identifies that person as a member of your family. Only then can you record the name on the family tree at the front or back of this book.

The detective work involved in tracing your family tree is its own reward, yet small when compared with the satisfaction of getting to know your family by means of undiscovered legend, quirky anecdote, and buried secret. So always be on the lookout for new tales to increase your collection. Trivial yet fascinating, such details bring your family tree to life and transform it into a unique heirloom for future generations.

ALL ABOUT YOU

Significant details

NAME & NICKNAMES

DATE, PLACE & TIME OF BIRTH

DISTINGUISHING FEATURES

PHOTOGRAPH

TYPICAL FAMILY CHARACTERISTICS

CLOSEST FRIENDS

Childhood

CHILDHOOD HOME

EARLIEST MEMORY OF MOTHER & FATHER

MOST & LEAST LIKED FOODS

FAVORITE GAMES & TOYS

BEST FRIENDS

FAMILY PETS

FIRST SCHOOL

Teenage years

SECOND SCHOOL

FAVORITE SUBJECTS & TEACHERS

SPECIAL FRIENDS

FAVORITE HOBBIES & PASTIMES

FIRST DATE

FAVORITE SINGER OR GROUP & SONG

Adulthood

FURTHER EDUCATION

FIRST JOB

FIRST PAYCHECK

FIRST HOME OF YOUR OWN

FAVORITE ACTIVITIES

FAVORITE VACATION SPOTS

MAJOR ACHIEVEMENTS & AMBITIONS

ALL ABOUT YOUR HUSBAND

Significant details

NAME & NICKNAMES

DATE, PLACE & TIME OF BIRTH

DISTINGUISHING FEATURES

TYPICAL FAMILY CHARACTERISTICS

CLOSEST FRIENDS

PHOTOGRAPH

Childhood

CHILDHOOD HOME

EARLIEST MEMORY OF MOTHER & FATHER

MOST & LEAST LIKED FOODS

FAVORITE GAMES & TOYS

BEST FRIENDS

FAMILY PETS

FIRST SCHOOL

Teenage years

SECOND SCHOOL

FAVORITE SUBJECTS & TEACHERS

SPECIAL FRIENDS

FAVORITE HOBBIES & PASTIMES

FIRST DATE

FAVORITE SINGER OR GROUP & SONG

Adulthood

FURTHER EDUCATION

FIRST JOB

FIRST PAYCHECK

FIRST HOME OF HIS OWN

FAVORITE ACTIVITIES

FAVORITE VACATION SPOTS

MAJOR ACHIEVEMENTS & AMBITIONS

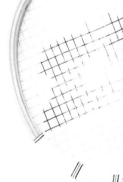

Your MARRIAGE

HOW YOU & YOUR PARTNER FIRST MET

WHEN & HOW HE PROPOSED

The wedding

DATE, PLACE & TIME OF CEREMONY

WHAT THE WEATHER WAS LIKE

BEST MAN & USHERS

BRIDESMAIDS, MAID OF HONOR & ATTENDANTS

WEDDING & GOING-AWAY OUTFITS

RECEPTION SITE

RECEPTION MENU

MEMORABLE MOMENTS OF THE CEREMONY

HONEYMOON MEMORIES

PHOTOGRAPH

PHOTOGRAPH

Your life together

YOUR FIRST HOME

YOUR HOME NOW

YOUR FIRST MARRIED YEAR

HOPES, DREAMS & AMBITIONS

YOUR FIRST ANNIVERSARY

$\mathscr{Y}$OUR CHILDREN

First child

NAME & NICKNAMES

DATE, PLACE & TIME OF BIRTH

SPECIAL MEMORIES OF THE BIRTH

FIRST WORDS

FIRST STEPS

FIRST BIRTHDAY

FIRST DAY AT SCHOOL

Second child

NAME & NICKNAMES

DATE, PLACE & TIME OF BIRTH

SPECIAL MEMORIES OF THE BIRTH

FIRST WORDS

FIRST STEPS

FIRST BIRTHDAY

FIRST DAY AT SCHOOL

PHOTOGRAPH

PHOTOGRAPH

PHOTOGRAPH

Third child

NAME & NICKNAMES

FIRST STEPS

DATE, PLACE & TIME OF BIRTH

FIRST BIRTHDAY

FIRST DAY AT SCHOOL

SPECIAL MEMORIES OF THE BIRTH

Names of other children

FIRST WORDS

*Y*OUR MOTHER

Significant details

NAME & NICKNAMES

DATE, PLACE & TIME OF BIRTH

PHOTOGRAPH

DISTINGUISHING FEATURES

TYPICAL FAMILY CHARACTERISTICS

BEST FRIENDS

Childhood

CHILDHOOD HOME

SIGNIFICANT MEMORIES OF PARENTS

FAVORITE GAMES & PASTIMES

FAMILY PETS

MOST SIGNIFICANT CHILDHOOD MEMORY

MEMORIES OF SCHOOL & TEACHERS

Adulthood

FURTHER EDUCATION

FIRST JOB

FIRST PAYCHECK

FIRST MEETING WITH YOUR FATHER

FIRST IMPRESSION OF YOUR FATHER

DATE, PLACE & TIME OF MARRIAGE

HONEYMOON MEMORIES

FIRST HOME TOGETHER

FAVORITE HOBBIES & PASTIMES

MAJOR AMBITIONS & ACHIEVEMENTS

Her brothers & sisters

NAME

DATE OF BIRTH

CHILDREN

NAME

DATE OF BIRTH

CHILDREN

NAME

DATE OF BIRTH

CHILDREN

NAME

DATE OF BIRTH

CHILDREN

NAMES OF OTHER SIBLINGS

Your FATHER

Significant details

NAME & NICKNAMES

DATE, PLACE & TIME OF BIRTH

DISTINGUISHING FEATURES

TYPICAL FAMILY CHARACTERISTICS

BEST FRIENDS

Childhood

CHILDHOOD HOME

SIGNIFICANT MEMORIES OF PARENTS

FAVORITE GAMES & PASTIMES

FAMILY PETS

MOST SIGNIFICANT CHILDHOOD MEMORY

SPECIAL FRIENDS

MEMORIES OF SCHOOL & TEACHERS

Adulthood

FURTHER EDUCATION

FIRST JOB

FIRST PAYCHECK

WHEN & HOW HE PROPOSED

FIRST IMPRESSION OF YOUR MOTHER

FAVORITE SPORTS & HOBBIES

FAVORITE CITY & VACATION

MEMORABLE EVENTS

MAJOR AMBITIONS & ACHIEVEMENTS

His brothers & sisters

NAME

DATE OF BIRTH

CHILDREN

PHOTOGRAPH

NAME

DATE OF BIRTH

CHILDREN

NAME

DATE OF BIRTH

CHILDREN

NAME

DATE OF BIRTH

CHILDREN

NAMES OF OTHER SIBLINGS

*Y*OUR BROTHERS & SISTERS

Brother

NAME & NICKNAMES

DATE OF BIRTH

TYPICAL FAMILY CHARACTERISTICS

SIGNIFICANT CHILDHOOD MEMORIES

WIFE

HOME

His children

NAMES & NICKNAMES

DATES OF BIRTH

PHOTOGRAPH

PHOTOGRAPH

Brother

NAME & NICKNAMES

DATE OF BIRTH

TYPICAL FAMILY CHARACTERISTICS

SIGNIFICANT CHILDHOOD MEMORIES

WIFE

HOME

His children

NAMES & NICKNAMES

DATES OF BIRTH

Sister

NAME & NICKNAMES

DATE OF BIRTH

TYPICAL FAMILY CHARACTERISTICS

SIGNIFICANT CHILDHOOD MEMORIES

HUSBAND

HOME

Sister

NAME & NICKNAMES

DATE OF BIRTH

TYPICAL FAMILY CHARACTERISTICS

SIGNIFICANT CHILDHOOD MEMORIES

HUSBAND

HOME

PHOTOGRAPH

Her children

NAMES & NICKNAMES

DATES OF BIRTH

Her children

NAMES & NICKNAMES

DATES OF BIRTH

PHOTOGRAPH

Your other close relatives

On your mother's side

NAME & NICKNAMES

DATE OF BIRTH

HOW RELATED

CHILDREN

SPECIAL FAMILY MEMORIES

NAME & NICKNAMES

DATE OF BIRTH

HOW RELATED

CHILDREN

SPECIAL FAMILY MEMORIES

PHOTOGRAPH

NAME & NICKNAMES

DATE OF BIRTH

HOW RELATED

CHILDREN

SPECIAL FAMILY MEMORIES

NAME & NICKNAMES

DATE OF BIRTH

HOW RELATED

CHILDREN

SPECIAL FAMILY MEMORIES

On your father's side

NAME & NICKNAMES

DATE OF BIRTH

HOW RELATED

CHILDREN

SPECIAL FAMILY MEMORIES

NAME & NICKNAMES

DATE OF BIRTH

HOW RELATED

CHILDREN

SPECIAL FAMILY MEMORIES

PHOTOGRAPH

NAME & NICKNAMES

DATE OF BIRTH

HOW RELATED

CHILDREN

SPECIAL FAMILY MEMORIES

NAME & NICKNAMES

DATE OF BIRTH

HOW RELATED

CHILDREN

SPECIAL FAMILY MEMORIES

Your MATERNAL GRANDMOTHER

Significant details

NAME & NICKNAMES

DATE & PLACE OF BIRTH

DISTINGUISHING FEATURES

TYPICAL FAMILY CHARACTERISTICS

Childhood

CHILDHOOD HOME

FAVORITE ACTIVITIES

MEMORIES OF PARENTS

MEMORIES OF SCHOOL

PHOTOGRAPH

Adulthood

FURTHER EDUCATION

FIRST JOB

FIRST PAYCHECK

FIRST MEETING WITH YOUR GRANDFATHER

FIRST IMPRESSION OF YOUR GRANDFATHER

FIRST HOME

FAVORITE HOBBIES & PASTIMES

MEMORABLE JOURNEYS & EVENTS

Her brothers & sisters

NAME

DATE OF BIRTH

CHILDREN

NAME

DATE OF BIRTH

CHILDREN

NAME

DATE OF BIRTH

CHILDREN

NAME

DATE OF BIRTH

CHILDREN

NAMES OF OTHER SIBLINGS

Your MATERNAL GRANDFATHER

Significant details

NAME & NICKNAMES

DATE & PLACE OF BIRTH

DISTINGUISHING FEATURES

TYPICAL FAMILY CHARACTERISTICS

PHOTOGRAPH

Childhood

CHILDHOOD HOME

FAVORITE ACTIVITIES

MEMORIES OF PARENTS

MEMORIES OF SCHOOL

Adulthood

FURTHER EDUCATION

FIRST JOB

FIRST PAYCHECK

WHEN & HOW HE PROPOSED

FIRST IMPRESSION OF YOUR GRANDMOTHER

HONEYMOON MEMORIES

GRANDPARENTS' HOME YOU REMEMBER

FAVORITE HOBBIES & PASTIMES

MEMORABLE JOURNEYS & EVENTS

His brothers & sisters

NAME

DATE OF BIRTH

CHILDREN

NAME

DATE OF BIRTH

CHILDREN

NAME

DATE OF BIRTH

CHILDREN

NAME

DATE OF BIRTH

CHILDREN

NAMES OF OTHER SIBLINGS

*Y*OUR PATERNAL GRANDMOTHER

Significant details

NAME & NICKNAMES

DATE & PLACE OF BIRTH

DISTINGUISHING FEATURES

TYPICAL FAMILY CHARACTERISTICS

Childhood

CHILDHOOD HOME

FAVORITE ACTIVITIES

MEMORIES OF PARENTS

MEMORIES OF SCHOOL

PHOTOGRAPH

Adulthood

FURTHER EDUCATION

FIRST JOB

FIRST PAYCHECK

FIRST MEETING WITH YOUR GRANDFATHER

FIRST IMPRESSION OF YOUR GRANDFATHER

FIRST HOME

FAVORITE HOBBIES & PASTIMES

MEMORABLE JOURNEYS & EVENTS

Her brothers & sisters

NAME

DATE OF BIRTH

CHILDREN

NAME

DATE OF BIRTH

CHILDREN

NAME

DATE OF BIRTH

CHILDREN

NAME

DATE OF BIRTH

CHILDREN

NAMES OF OTHER SIBLINGS

$\mathscr{Y}$OUR PATERNAL GRANDFATHER

Significant details

NAME & NICKNAMES

DATE & PLACE OF BIRTH

DISTINGUISHING FEATURES

TYPICAL FAMILY CHARACTERISTICS

Childhood

CHILDHOOD HOME

FAVORITE ACTIVITIES

MEMORIES OF PARENTS

MEMORIES OF SCHOOL

Adulthood

FURTHER EDUCATION

FIRST JOB

FIRST PAYCHECK

WHEN & HOW HE PROPOSED

FIRST IMPRESSION OF YOUR GRANDMOTHER

HONEYMOON MEMORIES

PHOTOGRAPH

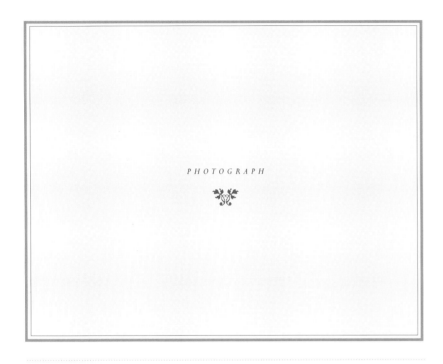

GRANDPARENTS' HOME YOU REMEMBER

FAVORITE HOBBIES & PASTIMES

MEMORABLE TRAVEL

His brothers & sisters

NAME

DATE OF BIRTH

CHILDREN

NAME

DATE OF BIRTH

CHILDREN

NAME

DATE OF BIRTH

CHILDREN

NAME

DATE OF BIRTH

CHILDREN

NAMES OF OTHER SIBLINGS

$\mathcal{Y}$OUR GREAT-GRANDPARENTS

Maternal grandmother's mother

NAME

DATE & PLACE OF BIRTH

WHEN & WHERE MARRIED

PHOTOGRAPH

Maternal grandfather's mother

NAME

DATE & PLACE OF BIRTH

WHEN & WHERE MARRIED

PHOTOGRAPH

Maternal grandmother's father

NAME

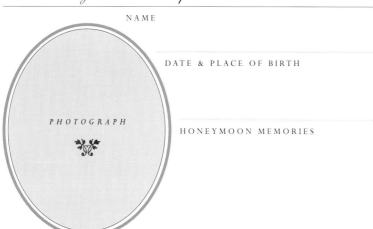

PHOTOGRAPH

DATE & PLACE OF BIRTH

HONEYMOON MEMORIES

Maternal grandfather's father

NAME

PHOTOGRAPH

DATE & PLACE OF BIRTH

HONEYMOON MEMORIES

Paternal grandmother's mother

NAME

DATE & PLACE OF BIRTH

WHEN & WHERE MARRIED

PHOTOGRAPH

Paternal grandfather's mother

NAME

DATE & PLACE OF BIRTH

WHEN & WHERE MARRIED

PHOTOGRAPH

Paternal grandmother's father

NAME

PHOTOGRAPH

DATE & PLACE OF BIRTH

HONEYMOON MEMORIES

Paternal grandfather's father

NAME

PHOTOGRAPH

DATE & PLACE OF BIRTH

HONEYMOON MEMORIES

$\mathcal{Y}$OUR OTHER ANCESTORS

Mother's ancestors

NAME

NAME

DATE & PLACE OF BIRTH

DATE & PLACE OF BIRTH

HOW RELATED

HOW RELATED

DATE OF DEATH

DATE OF DEATH

WHERE BURIED

WHERE BURIED

NAME

HOW YOU TRACED THEM

DATE & PLACE OF BIRTH

PHOTOGRAPH

HOW RELATED

STORIES YOU HAVE HEARD ABOUT THEM

DATE OF DEATH

WHERE BURIED

CHARACTERISTICS PASSED ON TO YOU

Father's ancestors

NAME

DATE & PLACE OF BIRTH

HOW RELATED

DATE OF DEATH

WHERE BURIED

PHOTOGRAPH

NAME

DATE & PLACE OF BIRTH

HOW RELATED

DATE OF DEATH

WHERE BURIED

NAME

DATE & PLACE OF BIRTH

HOW RELATED

DATE OF DEATH

WHERE BURIED

HOW YOU TRACED THEM

STORIES YOU HAVE HEARD ABOUT THEM

CHARACTERISTICS PASSED ON TO YOU

FAMILY STORIES & ANECDOTES

STORIES ABOUT YOU

ANECDOTES ABOUT FAMILY OCCASIONS

STORIES ABOUT YOUR BROTHERS & SISTERS

ANECDOTES ABOUT FAMILY HOLIDAYS

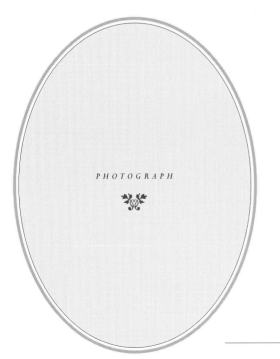

PHOTOGRAPH

ANECDOTES ABOUT FAMILY PETS

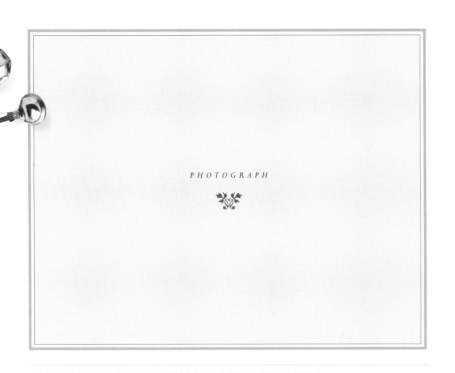

PHOTOGRAPH

STORIES ABOUT YOUR AUNTS & UNCLES

STORIES ABOUT YOUR GRANDPARENTS

STORIES ABOUT YOUR GREAT-GRANDPARENTS

STORIES YOUR MOTHER TELLS ABOUT YOUR FATHER

STORIES YOUR FATHER TELLS ABOUT YOUR MOTHER

FAMILY JOKES

 Your Husband's Mother

Significant details

NAME & NICKNAMES

DATE, PLACE & TIME OF BIRTH

DISTINGUISHING FEATURES

TYPICAL FAMILY CHARACTERISTICS

BEST FRIENDS

PHOTOGRAPH

Childhood

CHILDHOOD HOME

SIGNIFICANT MEMORIES OF PARENTS

FAVORITE GAMES & PASTIMES

FAMILY PETS

MOST SIGNIFICANT CHILDHOOD MEMORY

SPECIAL FRIENDS

MEMORIES OF SCHOOL & TEACHERS

Adulthood

FURTHER EDUCATION

FIRST JOB

FIRST PAYCHECK

FIRST MEETING WITH HIS FATHER

FIRST IMPRESSION OF HIS FATHER

DATE, PLACE & TIME OF MARRIAGE

HONEYMOON MEMORIES

FIRST HOME TOGETHER

FAVORITE HOBBIES & PASTIMES

MAJOR AMBITIONS & ACHIEVEMENTS

Her brothers & sisters

NAME

DATE OF BIRTH

CHILDREN

NAME

DATE OF BIRTH

CHILDREN

NAME

DATE OF BIRTH

CHILDREN

NAME

DATE OF BIRTH

CHILDREN

NAMES OF OTHER SIBLINGS

$\mathcal{Y}$OUR HUSBAND'S FATHER

Significant details

NAME & NICKNAMES

DATE, PLACE & TIME OF BIRTH

DISTINGUISHING FEATURES

TYPICAL FAMILY CHARACTERISTICS

PHOTOGRAPH

Childhood

CHILDHOOD HOME

SIGNIFICANT MEMORIES OF PARENTS

FAVORITE GAMES & PASTIMES

FAMILY PETS

MOST SIGNIFICANT CHILDHOOD MEMORY

SPECIAL FRIENDS

BEST FRIENDS

MEMORIES OF SCHOOL & TEACHERS

Adulthood

FURTHER EDUCATION

FIRST JOB

FIRST PAYCHECK

WHEN & HOW HE PROPOSED

FIRST IMPRESSION

FAVORITE SPORTS & HOBBIES

FAVORITE CITY & VACATION

MEMORABLE EVENTS

MAJOR AMBITIONS & ACHIEVEMENTS

His brothers & sisters

NAME

DATE OF BIRTH

CHILDREN

NAME

DATE OF BIRTH

CHILDREN

NAME

DATE OF BIRTH

CHILDREN

NAME

DATE OF BIRTH

CHILDREN

NAMES OF OTHER SIBLINGS

*Y*OUR HUSBAND'S BROTHERS & SISTERS

Brother

NAME & NICKNAMES

DATE OF BIRTH

PHOTOGRAPH

TYPICAL FAMILY CHARACTERISTICS

SIGNIFICANT CHILDHOOD MEMORIES

WIFE

HOME

His children

NAMES & NICKNAMES

DATES OF BIRTH

Brother

NAME & NICKNAMES

DATE OF BIRTH

TYPICAL FAMILY CHARACTERISTICS

PHOTOGRAPH

SIGNIFICANT CHILDHOOD MEMORIES

WIFE

HOME

His children

NAMES & NICKNAMES

DATES OF BIRTH

Sister

NAME & NICKNAMES

DATE OF BIRTH

TYPICAL FAMILY CHARACTERISTICS

PHOTOGRAPH

SIGNIFICANT CHILDHOOD MEMORIES

HUSBAND

HOME

Sister

NAME & NICKNAMES

DATE OF BIRTH

TYPICAL FAMILY CHARACTERISTICS

SIGNIFICANT CHILDHOOD MEMORIES

PHOTOGRAPH

HUSBAND

HOME

Her children

NAMES & NICKNAMES

DATES OF BIRTH

Her children

NAMES & NICKNAMES

DATES OF BIRTH

Your HUSBAND'S OTHER CLOSE RELATIVES

On his mother's side

NAME & NICKNAMES

DATE OF BIRTH

HOW RELATED

CHILDREN

SPECIAL FAMILY MEMORIES

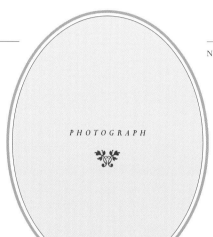

NAME & NICKNAMES

DATE OF BIRTH

HOW RELATED

CHILDREN

SPECIAL FAMILY MEMORIES

NAME & NICKNAMES

DATE OF BIRTH

HOW RELATED

CHILDREN

SPECIAL FAMILY MEMORIES

NAME & NICKNAMES

DATE OF BIRTH

HOW RELATED

CHILDREN

SPECIAL FAMILY MEMORIES

On his father's side

NAME & NICKNAMES

DATE OF BIRTH

HOW RELATED

CHILDREN

SPECIAL FAMILY MEMORIES

NAME & NICKNAMES

DATE OF BIRTH

HOW RELATED

CHILDREN

SPECIAL FAMILY MEMORIES

NAME & NICKNAMES

DATE OF BIRTH

HOW RELATED

CHILDREN

SPECIAL FAMILY MEMORIES

PHOTOGRAPH

NAME & NICKNAMES

DATE OF BIRTH

HOW RELATED

CHILDREN

SPECIAL FAMILY MEMORIES

*Y*OUR HUSBAND'S MATERNAL GRANDMOTHER

PHOTOGRAPH

TYPICAL FAMILY CHARACTERISTICS

Childhood

CHILDHOOD HOME

FAVORITE ACTIVITIES

MEMORIES OF PARENTS

Significant details

NAME & NICKNAMES

DATE & PLACE OF BIRTH

MEMORIES OF SCHOOL

DISTINGUISHING FEATURES

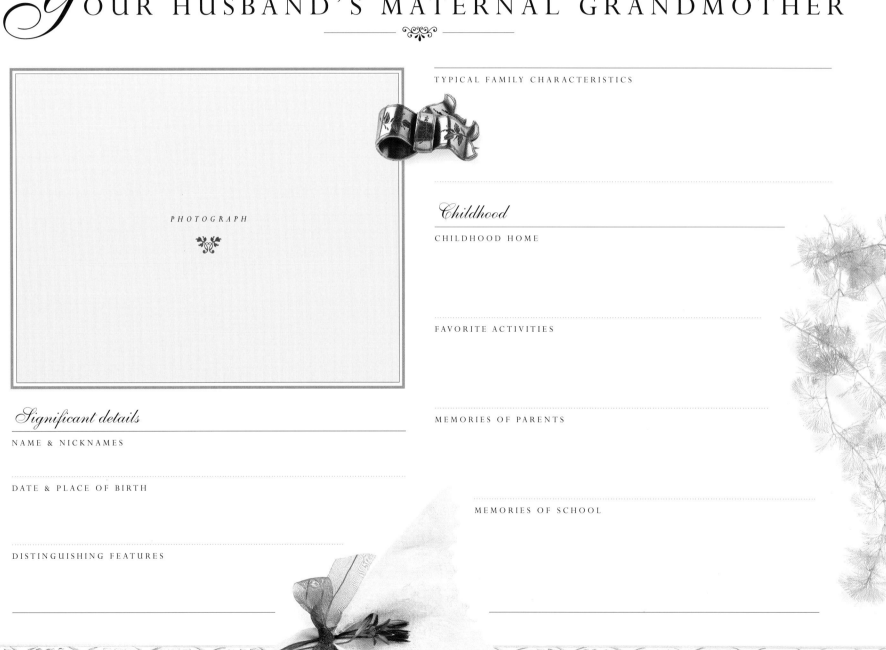

Adulthood

FURTHER EDUCATION

FIRST JOB

FIRST PAYCHECK

FIRST MEETING WITH HIS GRANDFATHER

FIRST IMPRESSION OF HIS GRANDFATHER

FIRST HOME

FAVORITE PASTIMES & HOBBIES

MEMORABLE JOURNEYS & EVENTS

Her brothers & sisters

NAME

DATE OF BIRTH

CHILDREN

NAME

DATE OF BIRTH

CHILDREN

NAME

DATE OF BIRTH

CHILDREN

NAME

DATE OF BIRTH

CHILDREN

NAMES OF OTHER SIBLINGS

Your HUSBAND'S MATERNAL GRANDFATHER

Significant details

NAME & NICKNAMES

DATE & PLACE OF BIRTH

DISTINGUISHING FEATURES

TYPICAL FAMILY CHARACTERISTICS

PHOTOGRAPH

Childhood

CHILDHOOD HOME

FAVORITE ACTIVITIES

MEMORIES OF PARENTS

MEMORIES OF SCHOOL

Adulthood

FURTHER EDUCATION

FIRST JOB

FIRST PAYCHECK

WHEN & HOW HE PROPOSED

FIRST IMPRESSION

HONEYMOON MEMORIES

FAVORITE HOBBIES & PASTIMES

GRANDPARENTS' HOME YOUR HUSBAND REMEMBERS

MEMORABLE JOURNEYS & EVENTS

His brothers & sisters

NAME

DATE OF BIRTH

CHILDREN

NAME

DATE OF BIRTH

CHILDREN

NAME

DATE OF BIRTH

CHILDREN

NAME

DATE OF BIRTH

CHILDREN

NAMES OF OTHER SIBLINGS

YOUR HUSBAND'S PATERNAL GRANDMOTHER

Significant details

NAME & NICKNAMES

DATE & PLACE OF BIRTH

DISTINGUISHING FEATURES

FAMILY CHARACTERISTICS

PHOTOGRAPH

Childhood

CHILDHOOD HOME

FAVORITE ACTIVITIES

MEMORIES OF PARENTS

MEMORIES OF SCHOOL

Adulthood

FURTHER EDUCATION

FIRST JOB

FIRST PAYCHECK

FIRST MEETING WITH HIS GRANDFATHER

FIRST IMPRESSION OF HIS GRANDFATHER

FIRST HOME

FAVORITE HOBBIES & PASTIMES

MEMORABLE JOURNEYS & EVENTS

Her brothers & sisters

NAME

DATE OF BIRTH

CHILDREN

NAME

DATE OF BIRTH

CHILDREN

NAME

DATE OF BIRTH

CHILDREN

NAME

DATE OF BIRTH

CHILDREN

NAMES OF OTHER SIBLINGS

*Y*OUR HUSBAND'S PATERNAL GRANDFATHER

Significant details

NAME & NICKNAMES

DATE & PLACE OF BIRTH

DISTINGUISHING FEATURES

TYPICAL FAMILY CHARACTERISTICS

Childhood

CHILDHOOD HOME

FAVORITE ACTIVITIES

MEMORIES OF PARENTS

MEMORIES OF SCHOOL

PHOTOGRAPH

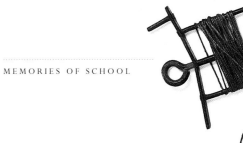

Adulthood

FURTHER EDUCATION

FIRST JOB

FIRST PAYCHECK

WHEN & HOW HE PROPOSED

FIRST IMPRESSION

HONEYMOON MEMORIES

GRANDPARENTS' HOME YOUR HUSBAND REMEMBERS

FAVORITE PASTIMES & HOBBIES

MEMORABLE TRAVEL

His brothers & sisters

NAME

DATE OF BIRTH

CHILDREN

NAME

DATE OF BIRTH

CHILDREN

NAME

DATE OF BIRTH

CHILDREN

NAME

DATE OF BIRTH

CHILDREN

NAMES OF OTHER SIBLINGS

*Y*OUR HUSBAND'S GREAT-GRANDPARENTS

Maternal grandmother's mother

NAME

DATE & PLACE OF BIRTH

WHEN & WHERE MARRIED

PHOTOGRAPH

Maternal grandfather's mother

NAME

DATE & PLACE OF BIRTH

WHEN & WHERE MARRIED

PHOTOGRAPH

Maternal grandmother's father

PHOTOGRAPH

NAME

DATE & PLACE OF BIRTH

HONEYMOON MEMORIES

Maternal grandfather's father

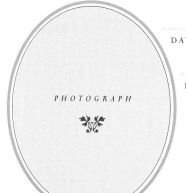

PHOTOGRAPH

NAME

DATE & PLACE OF BIRTH

HONEYMOON MEMORIES

Paternal grandmother's mother

NAME

....

DATE & PLACE OF BIRTH

....

WHEN & WHERE MARRIED

PHOTOGRAPH

Paternal grandfather's mother

NAME

....

DATE & PLACE OF BIRTH

....

WHEN & WHERE MARRIED

PHOTOGRAPH

Paternal grandmother's father

NAME

....

PHOTOGRAPH

DATE & PLACE OF BIRTH

....

HONEYMOON MEMORIES

Paternal grandfather's father

NAME

....

PHOTOGRAPH

DATE & PLACE OF BIRTH

....

HONEYMOON MEMORIES

Your Husband's Other Ancestors

His mother's ancestors

NAME
....

DATE & PLACE OF BIRTH
....

HOW RELATED
....

DATE OF DEATH
....

WHERE BURIED
....

NAME
....

DATE & PLACE OF BIRTH
....

HOW RELATED
....

DATE OF DEATH
....

WHERE BURIED
....

PHOTOGRAPH

NAME
....

DATE & PLACE OF BIRTH
....

HOW RELATED
....

DATE OF DEATH
....

WHERE BURIED
....

HOW HE TRACED THEM
....

STORIES HE HAS HEARD ABOUT THEM
....

CHARACTERISTICS PASSED ON TO HIM
....

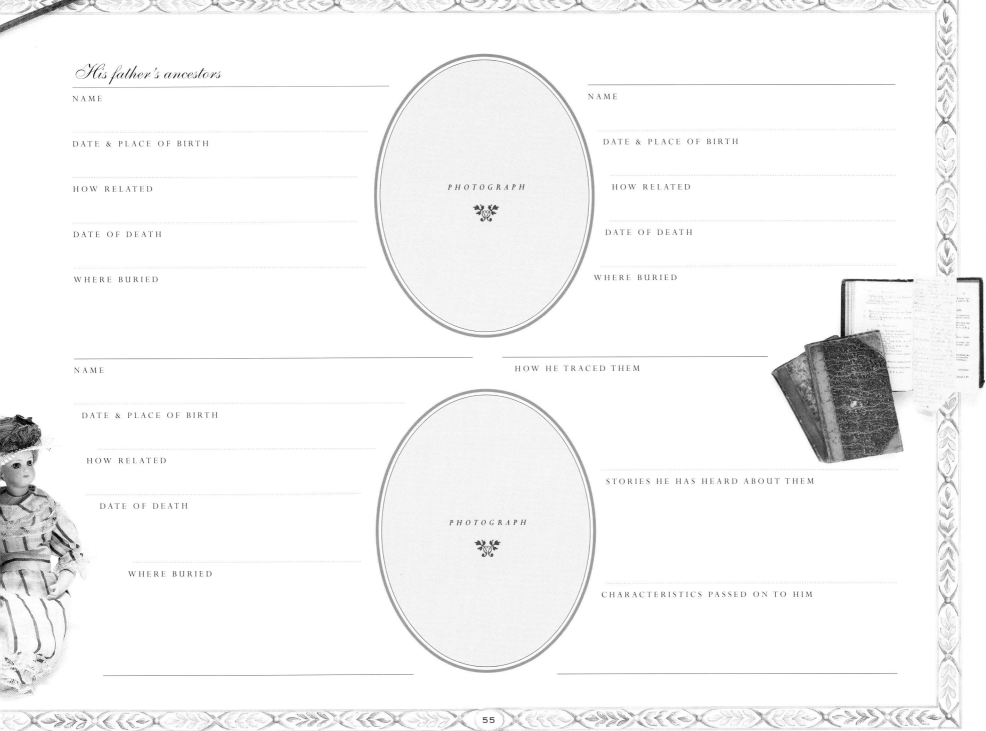

His father's ancestors

NAME

DATE & PLACE OF BIRTH

HOW RELATED

DATE OF DEATH

WHERE BURIED

PHOTOGRAPH

NAME

DATE & PLACE OF BIRTH

HOW RELATED

DATE OF DEATH

WHERE BURIED

NAME

DATE & PLACE OF BIRTH

HOW RELATED

DATE OF DEATH

WHERE BURIED

HOW HE TRACED THEM

STORIES HE HAS HEARD ABOUT THEM

PHOTOGRAPH

CHARACTERISTICS PASSED ON TO HIM

FAMILY STORIES & ANECDOTES

STORIES ABOUT HIM

ANECDOTES ABOUT FAMILY VACATIONS

ANECDOTES ABOUT FAMILY PETS

STORIES ABOUT HIS BROTHERS & SISTERS

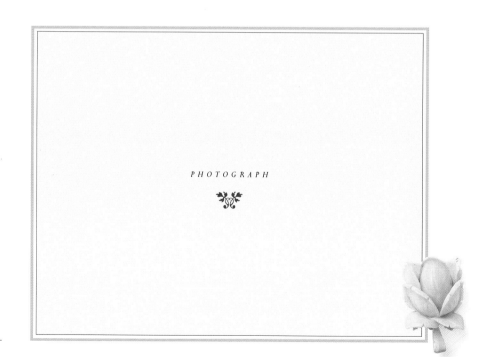

PHOTOGRAPH

ANECDOTES ABOUT FAMILY OCCASIONS

STORIES HIS MOTHER TELLS ABOUT HIS FATHER

STORIES ABOUT HIS GRANDPARENTS

PHOTOGRAPH

PHOTOGRAPH

STORIES HIS FATHER TELLS ABOUT HIS MOTHER

STORIES ABOUT HIS GREAT–GRANDPARENTS

STORIES ABOUT HIS AUNTS & UNCLES

FAMILY JOKES

FAMILY TREE

When you have gathered all the information you need, and have completed your research, write the names of your husband's family members – generation by generation – in the intertwining branches of the tree. This will create a beautiful and lasting visual reminder of his family history to pass on to your children.

FAMILY PHOTOGRAPH

GREAT–GRANDMOTHER

GREAT–GRANDFATHER

GREAT–GRANDMOTHER

GRANDMOTHER

GRANDFATHER

AUNTS & UNCLES

COUSINS

SISTERS

SECOND COUSINS

NIECES & NEPHEWS